PLANET PROTECTORS

Dominique Palmer
Illustrated by Komal Pahwa

Collins

1. The oceans are rising but so are we

My name is Dominique Palmer, and I'm a climate justice activist. Campaigners like me want to find ways to slow down climate change and help people affected by climate change. I have given a speech about protecting the climate at the Houses of Parliament in London and presented my arguments at the **United Nations** Climate Change Conference COP26. I was also one of the key organisers of the September 2019 climate strikes in the UK, where over 300,000 people came out to protest. I brought my passion for respecting and protecting the environment to the world stage, when I spoke to an audience of around 30,000 people at the Sziget Festival, Budapest, Hungary. My goal is to make sure that everyone knows they deserve a healthy environment and, for this, BBC1Xtra gave me a Future Figure award.

I am a proud member of the Stop Rosebank campaign – a group set up to halt the development of a large oil and gas field in the North Sea, off the coast of Shetland, UK. The Rosebank development was approved by the UK government in 2023, and an oil company started to build an oil rig there.

The Stop Rosebank campaigners took the UK government and the oil company to court and argued that the government's approval was **unlawful** because it hadn't considered the environmental impact drilling would cause. The judge agreed and the oil company had to stop work. We won!

I'm going to show you how I, and others, found the courage to turn our passion for the environment into action, and how you can do this too.

I've lived in London for most of my life, but I often visit Jamaica, a beautiful island in the Caribbean, where I have family. The first inhabitants of Jamaica named it "Xaymaca", which means "land of wood and water". The island has mountains, rainforests, **savannahs** and dry sandy areas. I love the feel of the sand between my toes at the beach, and the view of the horizon from the mountains. Growing up, I remember planting vegetables in the family garden, picking ackee fruit from the trees, and looking out for the Jamaican Tody birds and green parrots in the blue sky.

I learnt that there are "protected areas" in Jamaica. These sites are land or water, and they are home to lots of different plants and animals – some of which are only found on the island. There are strict rules about what you can and can't do in a protected area, and the number one priority is to look after everything that grows and lives there. This is good news for the environment, but then I found out about a different environmental threat facing Jamaica – rising sea levels.

Many people in Jamaica live near the coast; as the ocean surrounding the island rises, towns and cities are in danger from flooding. The change in sea levels is caused by the effects of climate change. The planet is getting warmer, and so are the oceans; when warm water expands it takes up more space. Ice sheets and glaciers are melting and adding more water to the oceans – all this extra water has to go somewhere.

I saw what was happening in Jamaica, but I lived in London and I didn't think rising sea levels affected me. What I didn't realise at the time was that climate change is something that affects *everyone*.

One day, everything changed for me. It was 2018 and I was at my local park in Lewisham. I watched with awe as a dazzling **murmuration** of starlings swooped overhead. They were beautiful, moving as one. They seemed so free, and sure of themselves. That was the moment I asked myself how I could make sure everyone in the future could enjoy sights like this.

Someone had put up a poster near the park. It said, "London is choking" and I wondered what it meant. I spoke to people in my area, and I was told that air pollution was a big issue in Lewisham – the poster was part of a campaign to raise awareness of this problem.

Toxic fumes, such as nitrogen dioxide, are released from cars and these can cause health issues, especially in children. It felt unfair that the area where I lived had high amounts of pollution, while other places did not.

I wanted to learn more about what was happening in Lewisham, and that led me to a bigger discovery. Climate change is caused by human activities, like burning fossil fuels: oil, coal and natural gas. These fuels are used for lots of different things from powering planes to heating homes. They're also used to power cars. When these fuels are burnt, the carbon produced mixes with oxygen and creates greenhouse gases, such as carbon dioxide. Carbon dioxide wraps around the Earth like a heated blanket, making the climate hotter each year.

So, what's wrong with the planet heating up? Many species can't adapt to climate change so they may become endangered. Climate change also causes rising sea levels, as I'd seen in Jamaica. As I did more research, I found out that other places were in danger, too. Islands like Tuvalu in the Pacific Ocean are low lying; the highest part of the island is only 4.5 metres above sea level. Experts predict that 90% of its land may be under water by the end of this century.

If you feel overwhelmed by climate change, you're not alone. Have you heard of "climate anxiety"? It means the fear or worry about climate change, and many young people are experiencing this. I understand this feeling; I have it too. Climate change is an urgent problem. We should all be able to breathe clean air, drink clean water and feel safe, no matter where we live, what we look like, or where we come from. The more I researched, the more I wanted to do something to protect the planet, but I didn't know what.

Then, in early 2019, I saw a leaflet about a climate strike that was taking place in London. These strikes were started by Greta Thunberg. Greta decided not to go to school every Friday – instead, she sat outside the Swedish parliament building with a sign that read: "School strike for climate". Her actions sparked an entire movement. Every Friday, more people joined her, and soon these strikes took the world by storm. I decided to join in.

In May 2019, I stood outside the Houses of Parliament. My hands were trembling as I held a sign that said, "Climate action now!"

People stared at me as I held my sign, and I felt a bit scared. Then I remembered something I'd read about trees while I was researching climate change, and this helped me. Trees communicate with each other through what is called the "Wood Wide Web". Fungi have underground threads attached to them, which connect to trees. In this brilliant network beneath our feet, trees share information, resources and the nutrients they need to survive. A climate change movement could be like this natural network. Trees are stronger together; I could be strong because

I was
part of
a network of
campaigners like me.

I spoke to **MP**s and councillors across the UK about declaring a climate emergency. It was important to me that our leaders understood the urgent need to reduce emissions and restore nature. The first step to addressing a problem is to acknowledge that there is a problem. Making my voice heard in this way built my confidence, and my friends in the climate movement helped me practise skills such as public speaking, writing, and deciding the focus of our projects. After a lot of hard work, and a fierce passion that never let us give up, we won! In May 2019, the UK parliament declared a climate emergency.

There's still more to be done, but this declaration made it clear that those in power understood that climate action is urgent.

I didn't stop there. On 20th September 2019, I helped to organise a UK-wide climate strike. It was the first general strike with adults and students. About 100,000 people showed up at the **rally** in central London! I made speeches and gave interviews, and people started to notice what I was doing. In December 2019, I was invited to speak at the United Nations Climate Change Conference in Madrid.

The United Nations is a global group formed by countries who work together to protect **human rights**, support climate action, and more. It holds a huge climate change event every year, where people discuss how to make change happen. This is where I met many activist friends, including some of the planet protectors in this book.

At the conference I delivered my speech and said, "Climate justice requires that everyone has a right to a healthy environment and to be represented in decision-making." I spoke to world leaders and asked them what they were doing about climate change, and I joined protests organised by Fridays for Future – the international youth movement started by Greta Thunberg.

We decided to draw eyes on our hands and sit on the floor in the middle of the conference area. The eyes were a message from climate activists to those in power: "We are watching you. Make the right decisions about our future!" At the same time the conference was happening, there was a climate strike in Madrid attended by 500,000 people. Half a million people marched through the streets. The energy and commitment from those who attended was incredible.

I continued to receive more **media** attention, and Sky News called me one of the UK's leading climate activists. In 2021, I attended the **TED** Countdown Summit in Edinburgh. The "brightest thinkers and doers from around the world" were invited to share their vision for a "better world". But when the **CEO** of global oil company, Shell, was invited to speak, climate justice campaigner Lauren MacDonald accused his company of causing "devastation" to communities around the world.

She told him he should be "absolutely ashamed" of how the oil industry was damaging the planet. I joined Lauren, and other climate campaigners and walked out of the event in protest. Outside the conference there were even more protesters who were unhappy that representatives from oil companies were at the summit.

In November 2021, I was invited to speak at the UN Climate Change Conference again. I joined a panel of climate change activists, including Emma Watson, Greta Thunberg, Malala Yousafzai, Daphne Frias, Maya-Rose Craig, Tori Tsui, Vanessa Nakate and Ati Viviam.

Amanda Gorman, the first-ever youth poet laureate in the US, participated via video link. She read her powerful poem about climate change called "Earthrise". We felt confident we were making a change and called ourselves the "Climate Justice League".

But after all this activity, I didn't see the results I wanted. I was anxious and exhausted, and I felt like giving up. This is when I realised that I needed to add joy into my activism. "Climate Joy" means holding on to hope and making planet protection joyful! This new mindset gave me the energy to continue. I helped plant up local community gardens and **rewild** areas to create habitats for birds and small creatures. I also spoke to young people in schools about climate action.

In the last six years, I've taken my message across the world but the most memorable thing I've done is to meet the young people I'm about to introduce you to. I've learnt from them, protested alongside them, and they've made me realise the power I have. There are so many ways to protect our planet. I hope that this book inspires you.

2. Goodbye plastic

Melati and Isabel Wijsen

Planet protector fact sheet

 Became changemakers at 10 and 12 years old.

 Founded Bye Bye Plastic Bags and YOUTHTOPIA.

 Melati's iconic quote: "Us kids may only be 25% of the world's population, but we are 100% of the future."

The people who have had the biggest impact on me are the young changemakers I've met. A "changemaker" is anyone who decides to create change. My friend, Melati Wijsen, has shown me that we all have power but we may need some help to find it.

Melati's journey started in the beautiful paradise of Bali, Indonesia, with her sister Isabel. Together, and as part of a people-led movement, they persuaded the government to ban single-use plastic. I met Melati for the first time in Paris in 2021, at the Change Now conference, and she told me her story.

As a child, Melati ran through Bali's lush rice fields, walked in pristine forests, and swam in crystal waters. Surrounded by this stunning natural beauty, she formed a connection with the Earth and learnt to care for it. She loved the beaches near her home and the ocean, and her parents taught her that every second breath we take comes from the sea. Melati realised that all of nature, on land and in the ocean, must be treated with respect and care.

Melati also learnt about *Tri Hita Karana*. This phrase reflects the balance between people, spirituality and nature. It means the "three causes of wellbeing", and one of these causes is harmony with nature and the environment. People who follow this idea live in harmony with the world around them by giving back to nature. This can mean planting trees instead of cutting them down or leaving water and food out for birds, so they don't go hungry – basically standing up to protect the one planet we call home. Melati made a promise to herself to treat Earth with care.

But something was destroying Bali's beautiful landscape. Something that threatened wildlife, sea creatures, water, food and forests – plastic. Melati said that Bali had become "an island of garbage". What was happening went against her belief in *Tri Hita Karana*, and she felt an ache in her heart at her home being threatened by human-made rubbish.

Bali residents, tourists, companies and organisations produce about 1.6 million tonnes of waste per year. Around half of Indonesia's plastic doesn't reach a recycling facility; instead, it's openly burnt, discarded in landfills, and dumped in rivers. All the plastic we throw away, such as drinks bottles and supermarket bags, ends up somewhere. Melati noticed there was plastic in the rivers, rice fields, the ocean and her neighbourhood.

Bali is located within an ocean current called the Indonesian Throughflow. Plastic waste from other parts of Southeast Asia is swept along this current and ends up on Bali's shores, particularly during the **monsoon season**. Plastic doesn't fully break down; it **decomposes** over a very long time into tiny pieces called microplastics. These microplastics end up in our water and our food. They're bad for nature and our health.

We throw out billions of pieces of plastic every year, which take 20 to 500 years to decompose. If humans continue like this, scientists predict that by 2050, the weight of plastic in our oceans will be greater than all the fish!

In 2012, when Melati was 12 years old, she decided that she could no longer accept her beautiful island drowning in plastic.

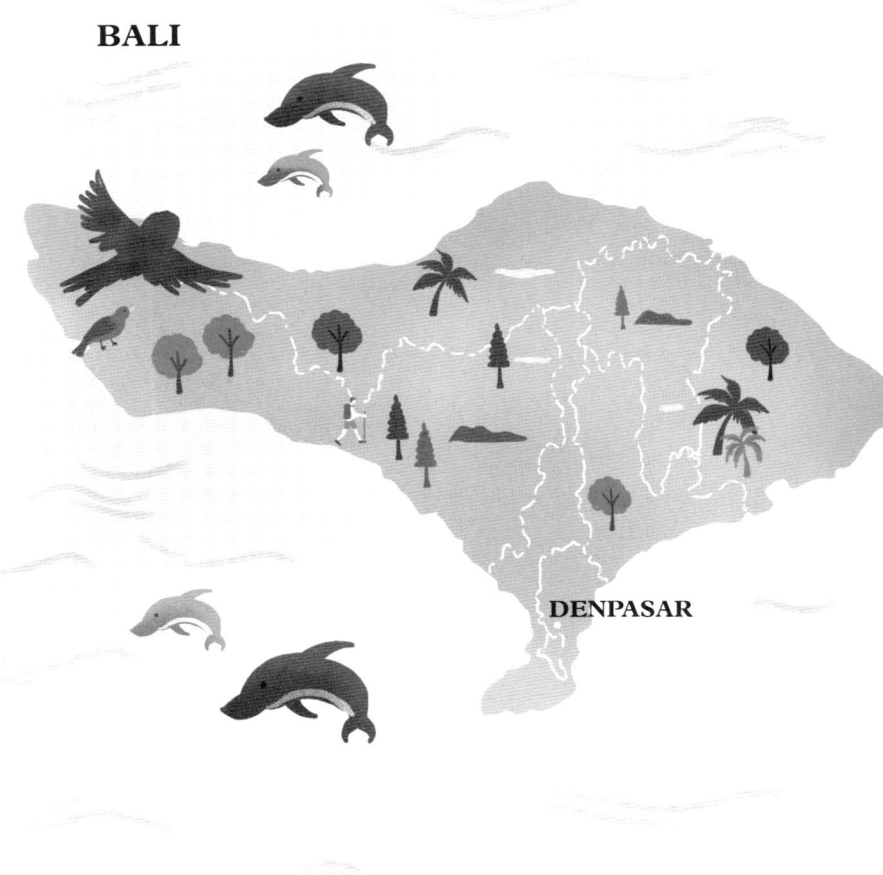

She didn't wait for permission to act, or listen to adults when they told her, "Wait until you're my age." She simply began. Now, she says that the thing she is most proud of in her life is having the courage to act, even when she was anxious.

At school, Melati was in charge of leading a clean-up of plastic bags. She told her classmates they could collect plastic bags, give them to organisations who would pay for them, and then give the proceeds to charity. However, she was surprised that some students weren't interested in the environment, or supporting charities.

Melati realised that not everyone understood just how much Bali was drowning in plastic. She wanted to raise awareness, so she decided to investigate and find out what happened to all the used plastic. There are ten official landfill sites in the country, but there are thousands of unofficial and unregistered sites. One day, Melati and a friend visited the biggest official landfill site called Suwung. When they got there, Melati could hear plastic crunching beneath her toes as she walked.

It was everywhere – mountains of plastic as far as her eyes could see. Birds swooped low, trying to find food, and cows walked around, desperate to find something to eat. Flies covered the air, and the stench of rotting materials filled her nose.

Tears spilt down her cheeks, and the stench made her sick. Melati said, "This was the first time I experienced a broken heart."

Once Melati saw the plastic landfill, she knew that she couldn't ignore the problem. Melati and her younger sister Isabel knew they wanted to focus on plastic pollution, but they also knew they couldn't change everything at once. So, they decided to focus on single-use plastic bags. Some countries had started to ban **non-biodegradable** plastic bags, but they were still filling up landfills and polluting rivers in Indonesia. Melati and Isabel knew that if other countries could ban them, theirs could too.

In 2013, at 12 and 10 years old, Melati and Isabel started a project called Bye Bye Plastic Bags. When they were asked why they created this project, Melati said: "It was the simplicity of doing the right thing for the right reason." First, they needed to get the attention of their government, and they thought a fasting protest could do this. The two girls got the advice of health professionals, and spoke with their parents, and decided to not eat anything from sunrise to sundown. Melati and Isabel said they would continue their fasting protest until the governor of Bali agreed to meet them.

Their story went viral immediately, and their actions were reported on all the local radio stations. Once Melati and Isabel had fasted for 48 hours, the governor called their parents and asked to meet the girls.

Melati and Isabel asked the governor to promise to ban single-use plastic bags, and he did! But after that, not much changed and Melati said she felt incredibly frustrated. Why was nobody acting? They met more politicians who gave them excuses like, "People aren't ready for change." So, what did the girls do? They set out to prove the politicians wrong and show just how many people *did* want change.

The sisters needed help to get support from across the country. Sometimes, as changemakers, we can feel as if we are the only ones who care about something. Before I took action for the planet, I felt that no one else cared about climate change. Many young people feel this way. However, I learnt that more people care than we realise, and often people care but are scared to say anything, because they also think they're the only ones!

This is something Melati and her sister discovered too. They asked other children in the area for help, and many of them were willing to act. The power of a small number of dedicated people started to transform Bali – the sisters had inspired a movement.

Melati and Isabel spoke to people in the street, in shops and in their schools. They created a petition to ban single-use plastic bags and hoped to get one million signatures. Lots of people in the community helped; Melati and Isabel made it fun by creating a competition of who could collect the most signatures. They held more events, educated people, and protested. Melati and the group gave out alternative bags, such as ones made from recycled materials. Although they were kids, this worked in their favour – children take a lot of interest in their world. They don't simply accept it as it is, and can be more willing to take a chance and grab opportunities that adults might not.

The Bye Bye Plastic Bags movement aimed for single-use plastic bags to be banned in the summer of 2013, but this didn't happen. Melati has since said that even when their ideas didn't go to plan, or they hit obstacles along the way, they were still making a difference. In 2017, Melati and Isabel, alongside others, organised the biggest clean-up that Bali had ever seen! After weeks of planning, thousands of volunteers joined them. Groups of people cleared rubbish from the beaches, running clubs picked up plastic on their trails, diving groups did underwater clean-ups and schools went out into their neighbourhoods to pick up plastic. Although the sisters became frustrated that the ban had not been implemented, they weren't going to stop.

In 2018, Bye Bye Plastic Bags became officially registered as a non-governmental organisation (NGO). These are organisations that are mission driven (like banning plastic bags!). If they make any money, it is reinvested back in to the organisation.

Finally, one day they woke up to amazing news:

In 2019, Bali banned single-use plastic bags, plastic straws and Styrofoam. Not only did Melati and Isabel succeed, but they also learnt lessons about friendship, leadership, how to deal with frustration, and more about their own country's culture. We gain so much from acting, even if we can't see the results straight away.

In 2025, Bali's government announced that they would convert the Suwung landfill site into an eco-park and waste power plant.

Activists like Melati and Isabel, along with the groups and individuals who pushed forward the movement to ban plastic in Bali, will hold the government to account for this. "We await the outcome to see if the government carries out its promises." They would like Bali to become trash free by 2027, and the movement to eliminate plastic waste is still strong.

Bye Bye Plastic Bags is now a national and international movement, working in 50 locations around the world. Melati and Isabel have spoken to over one million students and donated over 10,000 educational booklets to schools. At the World Economic Forum, 2020, Melati announced that she and Isabel had created a company called YOUTHTOPIA, an online platform for young changemakers. Today, they offer free changemaker training to empower young people across the globe.

3. Clean air and blue skies

Beau Boka-Batesa, Anjali Raman-Middleton and Nyeleti Brauer-Maxaeia

Planet protector fact sheet

- Became changemakers at 16 and 17 years old.
- Cofounded the youth organisation Choked Up.
- Determined to reduce toxic air pollution.
- Iconic quote: "For us, campaigning is a lifeline, not a lifestyle."

Let me introduce you to Beau Boka-Batesa, Anjali Raman-Middleton and Nyeleti Brauer-Maxaeia, who launched a campaign to raise awareness about toxic levels of dirty air in London. Clean air is good for our bodies and keeps our lungs healthy. Dirty air can make it hard for us to breathe and can result in health conditions like asthma.

One of the major causes of air pollution is traffic emissions. Pollutants from vehicles not only affect a local area, but can travel far and wide. These pollutants also impact Earth's atmosphere. The atmosphere protects Earth from overheating, but pollution affects its ability to do this and leads to climate change.

Thankfully, there are people doing something about this problem. I first met Beau as part of the UK Student Climate Network while organising a climate strike. Later, my passion for reducing air pollution led me to meeting Anjali and Nyeleti. These three climate activists took action so that clean air could be a right, not a privilege. Anjali and her sister Malini lived close to the busy

South Circular Road in London. This is one of the areas which has the highest recorded levels of toxic air in the city. Scientists measure this pollution by capturing and reviewing tiny particles called PM2.5, which can harm our health when we breathe them in. In Lewisham, the PM2.5 level was higher than the World Health Organisation says is safe. One of Anjali's classmates, Ella Kissi-Debrah, tragically passed away in 2013. She became the first person in the world to have air pollution listed as her cause of death.

After this, Anjali was aware of what air pollution was, and how dangerous it could be. In 2019, the areas around all 98 schools in Lewisham measured levels of toxicity that exceeded the World Health Organisation's guideline limits. Beau, Anjali and Nyeleti decided that they could no longer ignore the dangerous air they had to breathe on their way to school, so they created Choked Up – a campaign to end air pollution where they lived. The trio were determined that no child would become ill from breathing polluted air again.

GREATER LONDON

Tackling such a big problem is difficult. This is why the campaign started simply, by raising awareness. Beau, Anjali and Nyeleti asked for help from the community, and Malini created their group's logo. They also met the Environmental Defense Fund, an organisation committed to climate justice, who loved their passion and ideas. This organisation agreed to give the Choked Up group some money to help with their campaign.

In 2020, the group put up road signs in Lewisham, Brixton and Whitechapel. The road sign campaign went viral, and the group was interviewed by local and national news and radio stations. They had achieved their goal of raising awareness.

Beau, Anjali and Nyeleti knew that the next step was for the government to act. In 2021, the London mayoral elections were taking place.

The Mayor of London has control over decisions in the city, including reducing air pollution. This was the perfect time to make their voices heard, but they were too young to vote. Instead of letting this discourage them, the group continued their road sign campaign and expressed their desire to meet the mayoral candidates. The road signs caught the attention of the candidates – the potential decision-makers. Choked Up hosted a two-hour discussion, that anyone could attend, to ask the mayoral candidates questions.

After this discussion, Beau, Anjali and Nyeleti wrote an open letter asking the mayoral candidates to commit to taking action which would reduce air pollution if they were elected. The group described the importance of clean air for our health, and the letter was shared widely: 100 doctors and nurses gave their support to it!

They were pleased that their efforts were being recognised, and learnt that a group of young people in Wales had been inspired to start a similar project called My World My Home. The Choked Up campaign had created a ripple effect of change.

After the mayoral elections, Beau, Anjali and Nyeleti continued campaigning. They went to events and spoke about what they were doing. In 2021, the Mayor of London extended the ultra-low emission zone (ULEZ). This is an area of the city where drivers must pay to enter unless their cars generate no or low emissions. In 2023, the ULEZ was expanded again to cover the whole of London.

GREATER LONDON ULEZ ZONES

Expansion by area and year

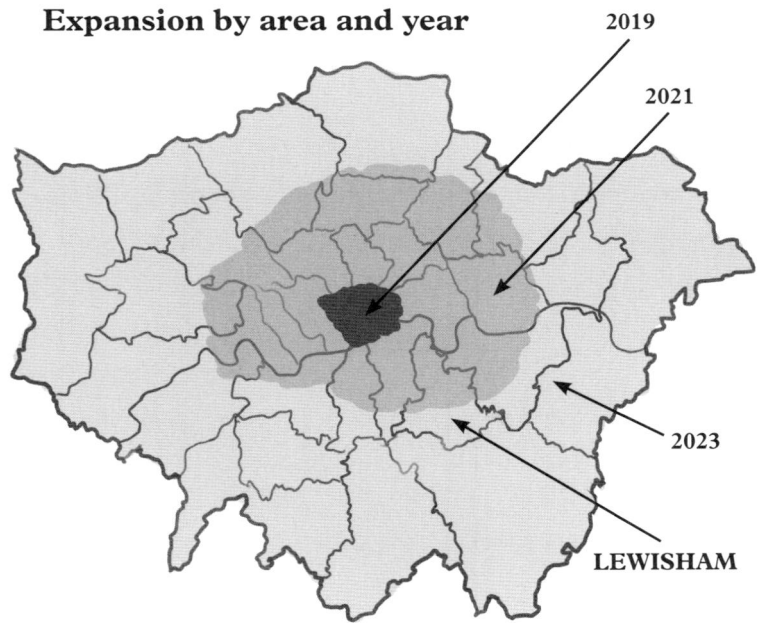

The ULEZ scheme has led to improved air quality for communities living near the busiest roads. Figures from 2023 show there has been an estimated 80% decrease in people exposed to below-safe levels of air pollution!

Air pollution still exists, but people like Beau, Anjali and Nyeleti show us that something can be done about it. They have inspired thousands of people, including Malini, who is now officially part of their campaign too. Now the group wants to expand, and it has met with people in Birmingham and Manchester in the UK.

Their next goal is to create a Clean Air Act – a law to reduce pollution from cars and public transport – across the country. Sometimes, you just need to get your friends together, make a plan and go for it.

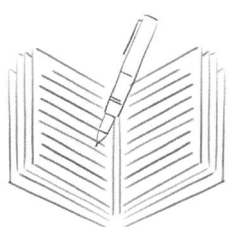

4. Education powers the future

Vanessa Nakate

Planet protector fact sheet

- Campaigns for gender equality alongside climate action.

- Founded the Rise Up movement.

- Founded the Vash Green Schools Project.

- Iconic quote: "We cannot adapt to losing our traditions, our cultures, our histories. We cannot adapt to extinction. We cannot adapt to starvation."

Vanessa grew up in Kampala, the capital of Uganda, with her four younger siblings and three cousins. A large percentage of the country is covered in glistening lakes and vibrant rainforests which are home to a diverse mix of animals, trees, insects and plants. Despite appreciating the nature around her, Vanessa wasn't aware of climate change or how that threatened the home she loved.

While she was growing up, Vanessa's parents encouraged her to follow her passions. Unlike many girls in Uganda, Vanessa was fortunate to have an education; she was keen to learn and joined Makerere University Business School in 2018. That's when everything changed.

While she was at university, Vanessa discovered how climate change was affecting her community in Kampala, and the whole of Uganda. Unbearable heatwaves, where temperatures reached 40 degrees Celsius, and unpredictable heavy rainfall leading to destructive floods were sweeping away houses and crops. When disasters like this happen to a country that relies on agriculture, the effects are long-lasting. Communities become homeless and families go hungry. People who rely on selling their crops become poorer. Families can't pay school fees, so their children miss out on getting a formal education.

Many countries in Africa, including Uganda, emit lower carbon emissions than other nations, yet Africa is experiencing the worst of its effects. This did not seem fair or just to Vanessa. She realised that climate change is the greatest threat facing the lives of people and she knew she had to do something about it.

Vanessa is quite shy, and it was difficult for her to find the strength and courage to become a changemaker. So, she took it one step at a time. Climate change is a huge issue that can feel overwhelming, so focusing on something that feels achievable is important. For Vanessa, this meant making a sign that included the message 'climate strike now' and standing on the streets of Kampala. In 2019, Vanessa stood in front of the Ugandan parliament and held up her sign in protest. She wasn't alone for long. Her siblings and cousins were inspired by her and joined in, demanding that their leaders act on the climate emergency. Everyone who joined Vanessa gave her courage to keep going.

AFRICA

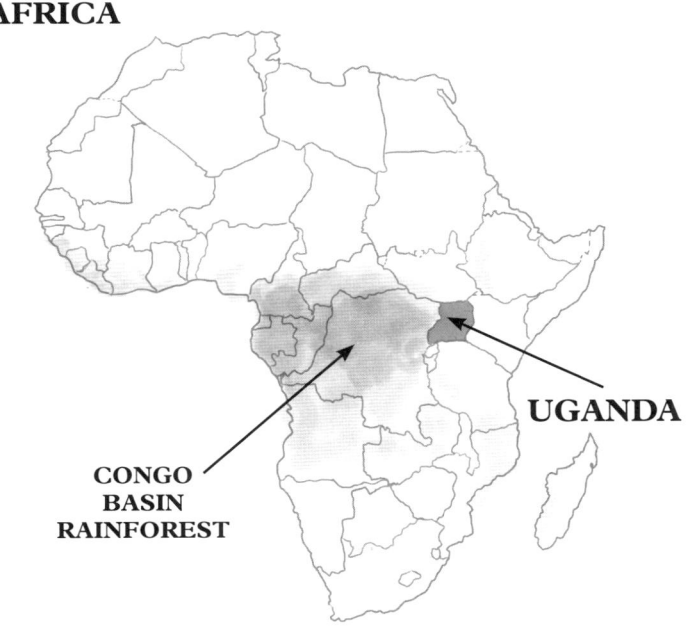

Vanessa read more about issues concerning Africa, and she discovered the destruction of the Congo Basin rainforest, known as the "Lungs of Africa" was taking place. The Congo Basin is the largest rainforest in Africa – it's home to about a million different animal and plant species, and millions of people depend on it to live.

This is because it provides food and shelter for the people who live there or nearby. It's around 500 million acres (that's about 250 million football pitches!) and has a rich and lush ecosystem. Species that live there include the critically endangered forest elephant, so it's essential to protect it.

Forests, soil and oceans, which absorb and store carbon dioxide, are called "carbon sinks". The Congo Basin rainforest is the world's largest tropical carbon sink and the second largest tropical rainforest in the world. It stores about 32 billion tonnes of carbon! Even though it's vital for the world, the Congo rainforest faces threats, such as deforestation. This is when forests are destroyed by cutting down or clearing a large area of trees, without planting new ones. Trees are usually cut to clear space for roads, charcoal production, building homes or office buildings, drilling for oil, or for farming. This practice harms people, as well as all the species which rely on the forests to survive.

In 2019, the Democratic Republic of the Congo lost over one million acres of forest. More than 158 million acres of the rainforest is under threat from new fossil fuel projects. Vanessa began to speak about the Congo rainforest crisis and encourage others to tackle climate change by planting trees and carefully bringing back wildlife that used to live there. As she spoke more about this, she gained the attention of the media and decision-makers all over the world. The young people standing outside the Ugandan parliament were growing in numbers, and Vanessa knew that others wanted to raise their voices too.

Vanessa had a plan to make even more impact; she decided to create the Rise Up movement, to bring attention to young changemakers across Africa. As this movement grew, she turned her attention to engaging more schools in Uganda. One solution to solving climate change is green energy. The use of solar panels provides an infinite source of energy, and solar energy doesn't involve drilling, toxic fumes, or environmental destruction which happens when using fossil fuels. Vanessa wanted to help more people use solar panels, so she started the Vash Green Schools Project in 2019. This project has already installed solar panels in more than 75 Ugandan schools, which means the schools no longer depend on fossil fuels for their electricity.

The Vash Green Schools Project caught the attention of the United Nations and Vanessa was invited to speak at the Climate Change Conference in Madrid in December 2019. After she stood on stage to give her speech about taking climate action, Vanessa gained more confidence. Her passion gave her bravery and strength. Everything was going well, and the Rise Up movement was doing better than ever.

In 2020, Vanessa was invited to speak at an event at the World Economic Forum in Davos, Switzerland. This is where world leaders, such as presidents, prime ministers, and decision-makers, are all in attendance. Vanessa demanded that large businesses, banks and governments immediately stop putting money into fossil fuels and, instead, invest in renewable energy. She and four other activists, including Greta Thunberg, were photographed outside the event. Everyone was desperate to get a picture of the young people who came to speak, but when she checked a news website, Vanessa had been cropped out of the photo and the words from her speech had been cut too. "It was like I was never there," she said.

Vanessa was angry at how she'd been treated; she'd been the only activist from Africa, but her contribution had been removed, and she felt as if the needs of a whole continent had been ignored. The Associated Press claimed Vanessa had been cropped out of the photograph because there was a building directly behind her. However, Vanessa argued the photo had been cropped because she is Black. The story went viral and so did Vanessa's response: "Erasing our stories won't change anything." Her message about climate change in Africa received global attention and Vanessa even did an interview with Hollywood film-maker and humanitarian, Angelina Jolie.

Becoming a celebrity wasn't important to Vanessa; she just wanted to make a difference. Her activism evolved. She began to speak about how vital education was for young girls and she continues to teach others the importance of positive change.

5. The lungs of the Earth

Helena Gualinga
Planet protector fact sheet
Born into a family of changemakers.
Front-line protector of the Amazon rainforest.
Cofounded the organisation Polluters Out.
Iconic quote: "Indigenous blood, not a single drop more!"

Our next planet protector is Helena Gualinga, and this story begins in the Amazon rainforest. The Amazon rainforest is often described as the "Lungs of the Earth" and covers 6.7 million square kilometres – twice the size of India. It's the world's biggest tropical rainforest and home to around 430 mammals, 1,300 bird species, 3,000 types of fish, 40,000 plant species and 2.5 million different insects. It's vibrant with lush forests, rivers and savannahs and provides people all around the world with food, water, timber and medicine. The Amazon stores 150-200 billion tonnes of carbon in its forests and soil, and helps to balance Earth's carbon and oxygen levels. It also recycles trillions of tonnes of rainfall back into the atmosphere – the trees suck up moisture from the soil with their roots, and release it through their leaves!

But the Amazon is under threat from climate change. Increasing temperatures impact the rainforest's ability to recycle rainfall. Without it, the rainforest experiences more droughts, forest fires and loss of species. It's also harmed by legal and illegal logging, when trees are cut down at an extreme rate. Land is cleared so farmers can graze cattle, make roads, use timber as material, or extract oil. Every minute, an area roughly equivalent to five football pitches is cut down. It's shocking, but people are fighting to protect the rainforests. This includes indigenous peoples, who live in the Amazon.

One of the countries the Amazon rainforest spans is Ecuador. Helena Gualinga lives here, on the Bobonaza River, Pastaza, and she is part of the indigenous Kichwa Sarayaku community. Around 1,500 people live there, and the only way to get to the community is by canoe or plane. It's a place where you could look up and see chattering groups of monkeys. Helena grew up drinking water straight from the creeks, growing fruit and vegetables, fishing and hunting. She loved to climb trees, and swim beneath waterfalls.

Helena has Ecuadorian heritage from her mother, Noemí, who is indigenous Ecuadorian and was the former president of the Kichwa Women's Association. Her father, Anders, is Finnish, and a professor of Biology in the department of Geography and Geology at the University of Turku, Finland. Helena spent time in Finland as a teenager, where she was able to experience new cultures and different environments.

In Ecuador, Helena lives near part of a mountain range called the Andes. Many streams flow down from the Andes into rivers such as the Bobonaza, and these eventually feed into the Amazon River.

If something happens to the water in the Pastaza region, this can affect the water levels in the whole rainforest.

Helena's grandparents told her that big floods only used to happen every couple of decades. But their village now floods up to four times a year because of climate change. She also learnt about logging, and its negative effects on her home.

In 2002, when Helena was born, an oil and gas company placed lots of explosives in the forest, so that land could be cleared for oil **extraction**. Neither the government nor the oil company had asked the community there for permission. The Ecuadorian government made decisions to make money, not to save the forest. In an interview, Helena said, "It was always part of my life that people were fighting for our communities. This was normal for me, that someone was trying to take our home from us."

More trees were cut down, and oil drilling destroyed huge areas of the Amazon and made the rivers toxic. Imagine waking up one day to find the beautiful glistening rivers you are used to swimming in have turned black, sticky and awful-smelling because of oil! Oil kills creatures inside the river and harms the people who live near it. Helena's people could not allow this to continue.

In 2012, when she was 12 years old, Helena's family, alongside the local community, fought back against the destruction of the forest. The Kichwa Sarayaku took the government to the Inter-American Commission on Human Rights, and they won! Although they were successful, there was still much more of the Amazon to protect.

Helena and her family organised protests and strikes. Several members of the Kichwa Sarayaku indigenous community lost their lives, including members of Helena's family, when they tried to prevent workers from large oil companies cutting down trees in the rainforest. Helena feared that, one day, she wouldn't have a home to return to. That's when she began to take action.

As a teenager, Helena began visiting local schools in Ecuador to educate young people and speak to them about how to protect their homes.

She spoke about the effects of climate change that the Kichwa Sarayaku faced, including forest fires and floods. She also joined protests, and more people began rising together.

In 2019, when she was 17 years old, Helena was invited to the United Nations headquarters in New York City. While she was there she demonstrated with other young activists and held up a sign that said, "Indigenous blood, not a single drop more!" When she was interviewed for a magazine, Helena told them, "I feel that this was not a choice, but I was born in the middle of this. This is an opportunity that must be used."

After leaders at the UN saw Helena's powerful statement, she was invited to the climate change conference in Madrid, Spain, the same year. This is where I met Helena for the first time! I was amazed at how she spoke to world leaders and called on the Ecuadorian government to stop granting permission to companies for oil extraction.

She called the Ecuadorian government criminal, for "still granting our territories to the corporations responsible for climate change".

In 2020, alongside environmentalists Isabella Fallahi and Ayisha Siddiqa, Helena founded the campaign group Polluters Out – a coalition of youth activists, adults and scientists.

Their mission was to make sure companies responsible for polluting Earth were not included in decision-making about climate change. She also cofounded the Indigenous Youth Collective of Amazon Defenders, alongside other young indigenous activists. The aim of the group was to protect the Amazon rainforest and advocate for indigenous rights.

In 2023, the Ecuadorian government held a vote. They asked the people to decide if oil drilling should continue in the Yasuni National Park in the Amazon. If people voted to protect their land, the government promised they would legally force the oil companies to stop operating in that area.

Helena and her community got to work! They created the Yasuni campaign and asked people to make videos to motivate the public. They also created a song about it that everyone could dance to. Helena said that it felt like the most exciting, important and stressful thing they had ever worked on together.

When the votes were counted the results were clear. The Ecuadorian people had chosen to protect their land. The power of people acting together stopped oil companies extracting an estimated 726 million barrels of oil from Yasuni National Park.

Helena said the effects of oil drilling and logging in the Amazon will take time to heal. She continues to teach others about the Kichwa Sarayaku people and the importance of protecting the rainforest.

6. Water is life

Autumn Peltier

Planet protector fact sheet

- Became a changemaker at eight years old.

- At 13, she spoke at the United Nations Assembly.

- Has been shortlisted for the International Children's Peace Prize three times and was a runner-up for the prize in 2022.

- Iconic quote: "I advocate for water because we all came from water, and water is literally the only reason we are here today and living on this Earth."

Over half of the human body is made up of water, and research shows that being in, on, or under water can make people feel more positive and reduce stress. Can you turn your tap on and drink from it? Where I live in the UK, clean drinking water is a privilege that most of us take for granted. But what happens when you don't have access to this basic human right?

This is a question that Autumn Peltier had to answer as a young girl. Autumn is an Anishinaabe indigenous rights activist and global water activist. She was born in Wikwemikong Unceded Territory, on Manitoulin Island, Ontario, Canada. Autumn speaks Ojibwe, and her home island is known as "Spirit Island" – an area that's important for biodiversity, and includes serene inland lakes, sand plain forests, wetlands, dense forests and sand dunes. It's also home to a wide range of animals, including grey wolves and black bears. Crucially, Manitoulin Island is the largest island in Lake Huron, which is one of the world's largest freshwater lakes.

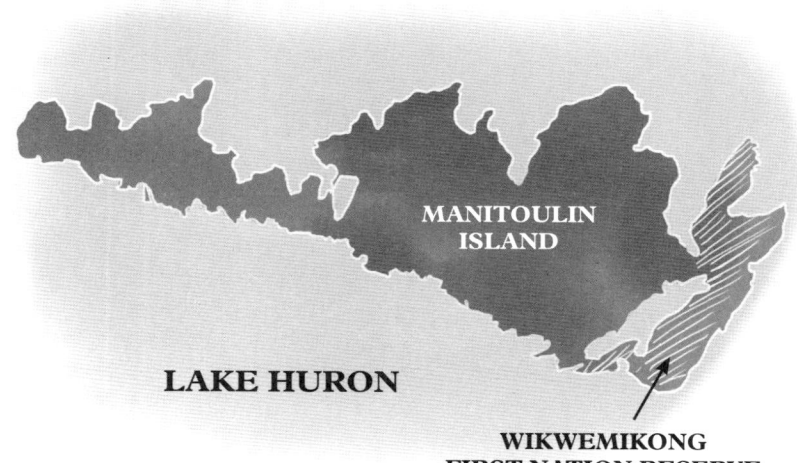

Autumn's great-aunt, Josephine Mandamin, was called "Grandmother Water Walker". She was the Anishinabek Nation's Chief Water Commissioner and founder of the Mother Earth Water Walkers. Over the course of 14 years, Josephine walked over 17,500 kilometres around the Great Lakes, holding a filled copper water bowl to bring attention to the polluted waters. In Autumn's community, an elder's knowledge is important. Her ancestors have an oral history, and pass down important information and stories through generations by word of mouth. But it wasn't until she was eight years old that Autumn truly began to understand why her great-aunt was a Water Walker.

Autumn attended a ceremony at Serpent River First Nation with her mother, where she saw something strange. Signs warned people of toxic, contaminated drinking water, and Autumn's mother explained that some people lived under a "Boil-water Advisory". This is when the government issues a warning that a community's drinking water is, or can be, contaminated by **micro-organisms** that cause disease. Where they lived, this warning had been in place for ten years. Autumn realised that children her age, and younger, wouldn't know how it felt to simply turn a tap on and drink. She knew that many people across Canada had access to clean drinking water, but her family didn't. Nor did families in other indigenous communities.

In the 1500s, around 200,000 indigenous peoples were living on the land that is now Canada, before European **colonisers** arrived there. The colonisers pushed the indigenous peoples out of their homelands, and the government forced these communities to live in settlements, called reserves, where the water was polluted. The First Nations peoples are a part of those who were moved from their land, and this is why Autumn grew up on the reserve of Manitoulin Island. This is what colonisation is, and the impact of it is still felt today. In many First Nations reserves in Canada, the population has to drink bottled drinking water because the natural supply is toxic due to pollution from oil and gas leaking from pipelines.

On Manitoulin Island, the community harvest crops for food and to make medicines. Autumn knew she had to do whatever she could to protect this way of life and solve the water problem. In 2016, she was chosen to join other indigenous communities in an Assembly of the First Nations to meet the then prime minister, Justin Trudeau. At 12 years old, Autumn presented the prime minister with a ceremonial copper water bowl to remind him of his duty to protect water. She told him she was unhappy with decisions that had been made to expand pipelines and drill for more oil. The prime minister promised Autumn that he would protect the water.

This moment was televised, and people across the world became aware of what was happening. From then on, Autumn was invited to speak about the importance of access to clean water. When she said, "We can't eat money or drink oil," people listened.

Josephine died in 2019, when Autumn was 14. Autumn wanted her great-aunt's work to carry on and, inspired by "Grandmother Water Walker", she continued to highlight the injustice of toxic water in her community. She was appointed the new "Water Walker" of her people – a title that was given to her because she had worked to bring global attention to their clean water campaign.

That same year, at the Global Landscapes Forum (a global community that promotes sustainable use of natural resources, like water), Autumn gave a speech about her time as a changemaker. She was determined that the Canadian prime minister would keep his promise to her. Today, 147 drinking water warnings have been removed! The Canadian government also aims to ensure reliable clean drinking water for future generations.

There are still people who live on reserves who can't drink their water, and over 30 drinking water warnings remain. Autumn was right when she said, "We all need to think about the planet and work together on solutions to reduce the impacts of human negligence." She was nominated for the International Children's Peace Prize three times, and a documentary was made about about her called *The Water Walker*. More work needs to be done to ensure clean water is accessible to Autumn's community, and she represents 40 Ontario First Nations with humility and passion. Her actions show that one person can educate the world and change people's lives.

7. People, not oil

Nalleli Cobo
Planet protector fact sheet
Passionate about stopping oil drilling.
Co-created the South Central Youth Leadership Coalition.
Iconic quote: "I fight because I believe that everyone has a right to breathe clean air."

Nalleli Cobo grew up in a Latino family in South Los Angeles, California, US. She lived with her mother, three siblings, her grandma, great-grandpa and great-grandma. When she walked around the neighbourhood with her older sister, she noticed tall, ominous-looking gates plastered with warning signs; it was the site of an oil well.

Many of Nalleli's neighbours and family members suffered from ill health. In 2010, when Nalleli was only nine years old, she started experiencing worrying symptoms: asthma, heart palpitations, nosebleeds and headaches. Members of her community began to speak to each other about their health; they knew something was wrong. Everyone could also smell rotten eggs – the stench was inescapable. Nalleli's health got worse. She suffered spasms and her legs would go stiff; her nosebleeds were so severe that she had to sleep sitting up. Finally, members of the community contacted a group of toxicologists – scientists who study the harmful effect that toxins and chemicals can have on people and the environment. They asked them to explain why the bad smells were occurring, and if this was making them unwell.

The smell was coming from the oil well site, which was located right across the street from Nalleli's house in University Park. Oil and gas drilling releases toxic chemicals and, in Los Angeles, these drilling sites are situated mostly in densely packed, poorer neighbourhoods where predominantly Black and Latino families live. Imagine going outside and seeing and smelling oil drilling next to your homes, schools and playgrounds. The scientists explained that the chemicals used for oil extraction could harm people's health, especially over a long period of time. This oil well, and others like it, was responsible for the emissions that caused climate change *and* making the people who lived near it sick.

Nalleli knew it was unfair that her community was so badly affected. She and her family and neighbours decided to take action. They wanted to shut the oil well down for good.

Nalleli and her mother started knocking on doors and asking local residents if the oil well was affecting their health too. They attended protests and meetings and Nalleli gave her very first speech at the City Hall. Her public speaking skills captured everyone's attention. People were listening! She became a leading spokesperson in the campaign to ban the oil well in her neighbourhood.

In 2013, Nalleli started the campaign "People Not Pozos" (*pozos* means "oil wells" in Spanish) and, in 2015, she founded the South Central Youth Leadership Coalition.

A news website wrote a story about the campaign, and it was seen by US Senator, Barbara Boxer. Barbara brought professionals into the neighbourhood to check on what was happening. The team entered through the ominous-looking gates Nalleli had spotted all those years ago. But they could only stay for a few minutes, as they started getting sick from the smell. Nalleli and her community had been living next to it for years!

Nalleli decided that enough was enough. The South Central Youth Leadership Coalition joined other organisations and they demanded that the city of Los Angeles stop oil extraction activities. They **sued** the city to demand more regulations for oil extraction – and won!

Despite the win, between 2015 and 2020, the state granted permission for more than 25,000 new oil wells. A report from 2020 showed that 2.17 million people in California lived less than a kilometre from an oil or gas well.

In 2020, when Nalleli was 19 years old, she was diagnosed with cancer. After months of medical treatment, she was declared cancer-free. Even after all she had experienced, Nalleli refused to give up, and returned to her campaign. That same year, her organisation had a big success. The oil well across the street closed down! Nalleli and her neighbours imagined a better future and created it. But it didn't stop there; the year after that, Los Angeles banned new oil wells and they considered banning already existing ones.

In 2022, Nalleli won the Goldman Environmental Prize for her campaign work, and the city of Los Angeles voted unanimously to phase out oil and gas wells.

Nalleli describes herself as just "a normal kid". She loves dancing, travelling, learning and makeup, but she found her passion and created change. Because she took action, the environment is a healthier one for her community.

8. The future is ours

By reading this book, you're already taking action for our planet. Education is powerful and what you learn can transform how you see the world. These incredible changemakers remind us that we don't need to do something big; we can all start small. We're the powerful force of change, and the future is what we make it. These planet protectors saw problems in their communities and did something to make change happen.

Hope is what we create together. I've learnt more about how problems are solved and met inspiring people through organising with others. Just being aware of changemaking is exciting! Although many of the planet protectors in this book captured attention worldwide and spoke at the United Nations, this is not a measure of success. There's so much possibility for the future. One where people have clean air and water, where everyone is safe, lives in dignity and can be joyful. And one where our ecosystems like the rainforests are thriving, with people living alongside them in harmony. Here are some things *you* can do:

- Start an environmental club at your school.
- Speak to your friends and family about what you've learnt in this book.
- Ask your parents/carers about travelling sustainably to school: walking, riding a bike, or taking public transport.
- Rewild areas of your garden or school.
- Participate in litter clean-ups.
- Build a bug house for your garden.
- Leave out food in proper bird feeders, especially in winter.

- Learn about your local environment: see how many trees, plants, birds and insects you can name.
- Continue learning about climate change and what people are doing to protect the planet.
- Take a reusable bag when you go shopping – don't buy plastic ones!
- Visit your library and read about the planet.

You have so much more power than you know. I didn't believe that I could make an impact on my own. Now my activism gives me courage, and joy. Every person who actively works to save this planet is brave, not because they act without fear, but despite it. As young people, we have so many ideas and so much creativity to offer. There are many solutions to ensure the wellbeing of our planet and the people who live in it. The future is waiting for us to dare to imagine it.

Remember, the oceans are rising, *but so are we.*

Glossary

CEO stands for Chief Executive Officer – the person in charge of running a company

colonisers people who take control of an area or country that is not their own

decomposes decays

emissions gases, particles or heat released into the air by mechanical things like cars and factories

extraction the process of removing something

human rights basic rules and protections that every person has such as the right to education, food and freedom of speech

media all types of communication and information, such as TV and newspapers

micro-organisms tiny living things that are too small to see without a microscope

monsoon season rainy period in South and Southeast Asia between May and September

MP Member of Parliament. Government officials who are elected to represent the views of the people living in the United Kingdom

non-biodegradable not able to decay naturally

rally gathering of people who are supporting a cause

rewild return something to its natural state

savannahs large areas of grassland with a few trees

sued started legal action against someone or an institution

TED stands for Technology, Entertainment, Design. An organisation that shares short talks from experts on lots of different topics

United Nations an international body promoting peace and security, that includes almost all the world's countries

unlawful not following rules or laws

Book talk questions

Whose story in the book inspired you the most?

What are some effects of climate change on our planet?

Have you noticed any consequences of climate change?

Have you ever participated in any projects to save the planet?

What can we do to help preserve our environment?

What does it take to become an activist?

What is the main message you took from this book?

What positive environmental changes do you want to see in the future?

What is climate justice?

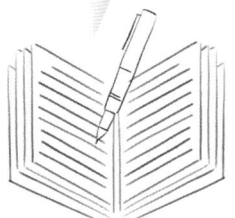

Which activists do you admire? Why?

Ask the author

What do you think is the biggest environmental challenge our planet is currently facing?
That people see the Earth as a resource to use rather than a beautiful, life-support system that protects us all.

What do you like to do in your free time?
Unsurprisingly, I like being outdoors! I love birdwatching and a good walk. Also, singing, dancing, fashion and crafts.

Dominique Palmer

What advice do you have for a young person who wants to be an activist like you?
To be an activist, you only have to act. What are you good at? What do you enjoy? What are the environmental issues near where you live? Is there anyone else you could team up with?

How can someone overcome climate anxiety?
Know that you're not alone. Talk to someone about it. Then start doing something! You will discover a community of people who share your concerns and are working hard to combat climate change.

Who else is transforming our planet that we should look out for?
Daphne Frias, Mikaela Loach, Lauren Macdonald, Wawa Gatheru, Elizabeth Wathuti, Xiye Bastida, Ati Viviam Villafaña, Hilda Flavia Nakabuye, Mitzi Jonelle Tan, Laura Verónica Muñoz, Rhiane Fatinikun, Nathan Méténier, Joshua Amponsem, Patience Nabukalu, Samia Dumbuya, Einass Bakhiet, Frances Fox, Tori Tsui, Joycelyn Longdon and Tolmeia Gregory. There are also millions of youth activists, who don't get any recognition, who I am so grateful for.

What are your career plans for the future?
I am working on some music, which is exciting!

What message would you like young people to take away from this book?
I would love young people to know that they have the power to be a changemaker.

What part of this book did you enjoy writing the most?
I loved discovering more about the rainforests, and about my fellow planet protectors.

Published by Collins
An imprint of HarperCollins*Publishers*

The News Building
1 London Bridge Street
London SE1 9GF
UK

Macken House
39/40 Mayor Street Upper
Dublin 1
D01 C9W8
Ireland

© HarperCollins*Publishers* Limited 2026

10 9 8 7 6 5 4 3 2 1

ISBN 978-0-00-878477-5

All rights reserved. No part of this publication may be reproduced, stored in a retrieval system, or transmitted in any form by any means, electronic, mechanical, photocopying, recording or otherwise, without the prior written permission of the Publisher or a licence permitting restricted copying in the United Kingdom issued by the Copyright Licensing Agency Ltd, 5th Floor, Shackleton House, 4 Battle Bridge Lane, London SE1 2HX.

Without limiting the exclusive rights of any author, contributor or the publisher of this publication, any unauthorised use of this publication to train generative artificial intelligence (AI) technologies is expressly prohibited. HarperCollins also exercise their rights under Article 4(3) of the Digital Single Market Directive 2019/790 and expressly reserve this publication from the text and data mining exception.

British Library Cataloguing-in-Publication Data

A catalogue record for this publication is available from the British Library.

Author: Dominique Palmer
Illustrator: Komal Pahwa (Astound Agency)
Publisher: Laura White
Commissioning editor: Holly Woolnough
Development editor: Zoë Clarke
Product manager: Holly Woolnough
Content editor: Selin Akca
Copyeditor: Catherine Dakin

Proofreaders: Sally Byford, Sasha Morton
Reviewer: Lisa Davis
Fact checker: Sasha Morton
Cover designer: Sarah Finan
Internal designer: 2Hoots Publishing Services Ltd
Typesetter: David Jimenez
Production controller: Sophie Waeland

Collins would like to thank the teachers and children at Grange Primary School, Southwark, for being part of the development of Big Cat Read On.

Printed in the UK

MIX
Paper | Supporting responsible forestry
FSC® C006032

Made with responsibly sourced paper and vegetable ink

Scan to see how we are reducing our environmental impact.

Get the latest Collins Big Cat news at
collins.co.uk/collinsbigcat